Life in a Fishing Community

Hélène Boudreau

Crabtree Publishing Company
www.crabtreebooks.com

Author: Hélène Boudreau

Editor-in-Chief: Lionel Bender

Editors: Simon Adams and Molly Aloian

Proofreader: Crystal Sikkens

Editorial director: Kathy Middleton

Photo research: Hélène Boudreau and Ben White

Designer: Ben White

Production coordinator: Katherine Berti

Production: Kim Richardson

Prepress technician: Margaret Amy Salter

Consultant: Heather L. Montgomery, DragonFly Environmental Education Programs

Front cover (main image): Boats in front of the Fisheries Museum of the Atlantic in the Lunenburg Harbour, Nova Scotia, Canada

Back cover: A young angler with a prize catch

Title page: Aerial view of the town of Lunenburg, Nova Scotia, Canada

This book was produced for Crabtree Publishing Company by Bender Richardson White.

Photographs and reproductions
All Canada Photos: Rolf Hicker: front cover (main image)
Katherine Berti: back cover
BigStockPhoto: p. 7, 12, 20, 28
Marc Crabtree: front cover (inset)
Getty Images: Aurora : p. 9; Grant Faint: p. 8;
    National Geographic: p. 6, 17, 29;
    Jeff Rotman: p. 11; Brian Summers: p. 4;
Istockphoto: p. 5
Topfoto: John Balean: p. 10
Len Wagg, Town of Lunenburg: p. 1, 13, 16, 18, 19,
    21, 22, 23, 24, 25, 26, 27
Amy Wentzell: p. 14, 15

Acknowledgments
Special thanks to:
Peter J. Haughn, Deputy Town Manager/Clerk, Town of Lunenburg, Nova Scotia, for providing images and information about his town.
Amy Wentzell, local Lunenburg photographer, and Len Wagg, Town of Lunenburg Office, for providing their copyright images.
Cover models Tanisha Burian, Terra Robinson, Devin Saumier, Dylan Saumier, Bailee Setikas, Shelbi Setikas, and Zach Sikkens

Library and Archives Canada Cataloguing in Publication

Boudreau, Hélène
    Life in a fishing community / Hélène Boudreau.

(Learn about rural life)
Includes index.
ISBN 978-0-7787-5072-7 (bound) --ISBN 978-0-7787-5085-7 (pbk.)

    1. Fisheries--Juvenile literature. 2. Fishing villages--Juvenile literature. 3. Fishers--Juvenile literature. 4. Lunenburg (N.S.)--Juvenile literature. I. Title. II. Series: Learn about rural life

SH331.15.B69 2009   j639.2   C2009-903596-0

Library of Congress Cataloging-in-Publication Data

Boudreau, Hélène.
    Life in a fishing community / Hélène Boudreau.
        p. cm. -- (Learn about rural life)
    Includes index.
    ISBN 978-0-7787-5085-7 (pbk. : alk. paper) -- ISBN 978-0-7787-5072-7 (reinforced library binding : alk. paper)
    1. Fishing--Nova Scotia--Juvenile literature. 2. Fishing villages--Nova Scotia--Juvenile literature. 3. Lunenburg (N.S.)--Juvenile literature. I. Title. II. Series: Learn about rural life.

SH445.B68 2010
639.209716'23--dc22

2009022918

Crabtree Publishing Company
www.crabtreebooks.com   1-800-387-7650

Published in Canada
Crabtree Publishing
616 Welland Ave.
St. Catharines, Ontario
L2M 5V6

Published in the United States
Crabtree Publishing
PMB16A
350 Fifth Ave., Suite 3308
New York, NY 10118

Published in the United Kingdom
Crabtree Publishing
White Cross Mills
High Town, Lancaster
LA1 4XS

Published in Australia
Crabtree Publishing
386 Mt. Alexander Rd.
Ascot Vale (Melbourne)
VIC 3032

Contents

A Rural Fishing Town

Most people live in big **towns** or **cities**. These are busy, noisy places where everything moves fast. Towns and cities are known as **urban** places. Other people live in small towns or **villages**. Here, everyday life is quieter and slower. There are fewer people and fewer buildings. There is less traffic. Small towns and villages are known as **rural** places.

▼ People who live, work, and play together in an area are known as a **community**. In urban areas with millions of people, such as Toronto, Ontario, there are many separate communities.

In rural places, such as the small fishing town of Lunenburg in Nova Scotia, Canada, there is just one big community. Almost all the people know each other. Most people are able to get everything they need within the town.

People need the same **resources** no matter where they live. They need food and clean water. They need shelter and **energy** for their homes and vehicles. They need jobs to earn money. Rural places are built close to these resources. This book looks at a small town that depends on fish and shellfish for food and a source of jobs.

Types of Fishing

Fish can be caught with a line and hook, as in **angling** for salmon. They can also be caught in nets as they swim along. Shellfish, such as scallops, are scooped up from the bottom of the ocean with metal **rakes**. Lobsters and crabs are trapped in metal or wooden traps.

▼ There is not an endless supply of fish and shellfish in the sea. Fishermen must follow fishing laws and keep to **quotas** or fixed amounts of fish.

After a fishing trip, the nets are emptied of fish then laid out to dry in the sun. The red rings on the small net are floats that keep it near the surface of the water. This is where most of the fish swim in the sea.

Fishing boats use big nets to catch fish at sea. Gill nets are stretched out in long rows underwater. Fish get tangled in the nets as they swim by. The nets have holes that are big enough to let smaller fish swim through. The young fish do not get caught and have a chance to grow. Trawler nets are like big socks that are pulled through the water. Fish get caught in the nets and are hauled aboard.

Types of Fish and Shellfish

A fish has a backbone and a skeleton inside its body. Sole, mackerel, and haddock are types of fish caught in the oceans of North America. Salmon and trout are also fished, but they can be caught in rivers and raised on **fish farms**, too. Shellfish do not have backbones. They have outer shells that are like skeletons.

▼ A fishmonger—a person who sells fish and shellfish at a market or in a store—holds up a big salmon.

Shrimps, lobsters, and crabs are known as **crustaceans**. They are shellfish that **molt**, or shed, their shells as they grow. Clams, scallops, and oysters are **mollusks**. Mollusks have shells that grow with them as they get older; they do not molt.

Fishing in North America

People have fished in the seas of North America for thousands of years. Today, fishing villages and towns are found on every coast. They range from tiny rural places to big cities with many **harbors**. There are only 631 people living in L'Anse au Loup, Labrador. Most adults in the village work at the shrimp-**processing factory**.

▼ In the early 1900s, catching fish was big business in Canada. Workers unloaded catches of salmon from flat-bottomed, square-ended boats. The fish were then carried by railroad and sold in cities.

A fishing boat at sea loaded with cod, flounder, tuna, bass, and many other fish. The boat sailed from Gloucester, a big fishing town on the coast of Massachusetts.

The town of Cortez, in Florida, has 4,914 **residents**. Fishermen from Cortez catch mullet in the Gulf of Mexico as they have done since the 1800s. The village of Klemtu, in British Columbia, Canada, has 450 residents. There, the **local** Kitasoo Native Band raises salmon in Klemtu's **aquaculture** farm.

Welcome to Lunenburg

Lunenburg in Nova Scotia, Canada, is a rural fishing town. It was **founded** by British people in 1753. Here, fishing and shipbuilding have always been an important part of town life. Lunenburg has a colorful waterfront and harbor. Like other rural places, it has schools, churches, a bank, grocery stores, and a weekly farmer's market where local people buy food.

▼ Along the waterfront are docks where boats can load, unload, and tie up. There are also wharfs or storehouses that sell fishing equipment and other supplies.

An aerial view of Lunenburg. On summer days, tourist buses, visitor cars, and boats of all shapes and sizes fill the waterfront of the town.

Lunenburg is also home to many businesses related to fishing and boat-building. Tourists come to Lunenburg year round and enjoy its many inns, restaurants, and shops. Visitors come for Lunenburg's pretty scenery, festivals, fresh seafood, and sites such as the Fisheries Museum of the Atlantic.

Daily Life

About 2,500 people live and work in Lunenburg. Some adults work in stores, offices, or at the harbor. Others work in the town's fish-processing factory. When children are not in school, they participate in activities at the community center, play at the recreation ground, or skate at the skate park. Some children help their parents in their stores or at their market stalls.

▼ At the recreation ground, childen play on swings and climbing frames, or play soccer and baseball.

Most residents in Lunenburg do their shopping in small stores. They must travel to larger towns or cities to visit shopping malls.

Lunenburg is a small town so it is easy to get around by walking or cycling. There is no public transportation. Residents often see people they know when the go into town. In the summer, many tourists visit and stay in the town. During this time, the streets, stores, and the waterfront are very busy.

A Lobster-fishing Family

In a rural town, there are many jobs to be done and not enough adults to do them. Everyone in a family has to help with the work. In Lunenburg, the lobster-fishing season lasts for only a few winter months. Often the weather is too cold to take the boats out.

▼ In the off season, the fishing boats are cleaned and painted.

On the boat, lobsters are taken from the traps and loaded into boxes. The fishermen wear thick waterproof gloves for warmth and to protect their hands from the lobsters' claws.

Before the season, the family cleans the boat and gets the lobster traps ready. Fish are cut up into tiny pieces and stored in freezers to use as **bait** for the lobsters. On fishing days, the boats are taken out to sea early in the morning and the traps are set. Later in the day, the traps are collected and the boats are sailed back to the harbor. The lobsters are unloaded and taken to the market.

On the Boats

Commercial fishing boats come in all shapes and sizes. At Lunenburg, boats used to fish for lobsters close to the shore are about 40 feet (12 meters) long. Lobstermen work in small teams of two to four. They make daily trips to collect the lobsters from their traps.

▼ Lunenburg fishermen go out to sea in all types of weather. As soon as they return to the harbor, they unload their catch.

▲ On small trawlers, fish that are caught are packed in ice or cold water to keep them fresh while on-board. About ten adults work on each small trawler.

Trawlers are larger boats used to catch fish far out at sea. The fishermen may be away from home for a few days before returning. Factory trawlers are the largest boats that fish near Lunenburg. They are up to 230 feet (70 meters) long. About 25 people work on board. They prepare and freeze fish on the boat. These trawlers stay out at sea for up to six weeks at a time.

When the Boats Come In

Not everyone who works on the waterfront of Lunenburg is a fisherman. The Harbor Master is in charge of helping boats **navigate** safely in and out of the harbor. Coastguards make sure boats follow the rules of the sea and keep out of each other's way.

▼ Boats that need to be repaired can be fixed at one of the Lunenburg shipyards. Then they are loaded with everything they need for voyage at sea.

▲ Working on big ships with a lot of machinery and heavy loads can be dangerous work. For safety, fishermen and dockers wear brightly colored protective clothing and hats.

On the waterfront, **dockers** help the boats refuel, set off, and tie up. They also unload small boxes of fish. Crane- and fork-lift operators help unload big containers of fish. On big boats, ice is used to keep the fish fresh on the way to the processing factory and markets. If the fish are to be taken a long distance, they are transported by truck or train.

At the Factory

Lunenburg has a 250-year history of fishing. Over-fishing in the past hundred years has left less fish in the sea. Many people that used to be fishermen now work at the fish-processing factory. Fish caught off the coast of Nova Scotia are brought here to be prepared for eating.

▼ Much of the work at the fish-processing factory is done by hand. Fish are cleaned and cut up. Clam shells are opened and the part that can be eaten is cut out.

Many people process the fish on a production line in the factory.

In the factory, fish are cleaned and cut up. Then they can be seasoned with spices or sauces, or dipped in flour and breadcrumbs and lightly fried to make fish sticks or fillets. Shellfish are cooked and their meat is removed and shredded. These fish products are packaged and shipped to stores all over North America.

Through the Year

In Lunenburg, there is plenty to see and do all year round. Winter is the fishing season, when the waterfront is busy with boats day and night. During the summer and early fall, the town comes alive with outdoor activities and events for residents, visitors, and tourists.

▼ During the summer art festival, musicians come from neighboring towns to play at bandstands.

Like many rural places, Lunenburg has a few big events each year. Everyone in the town gets involved. They rehearse shows and plays and make things to sell. The Waterfront and Seafood Festival takes place in September. Big sailing ships from all over North America visit the harbor for people to explore.

Changing Lifestyle

The town of Lunenburg is a mixture of old and new. All the old buildings—houses, stores, barns, warehouses, and shipbuilding yards—are made of wood. Some new buildings, such as the fish-processing factory and small offices, are made of brick, concrete, and steel. The rural look and feel of the town is changing.

▼ Many local people keep up the old **traditions**. Here they are racing small wooden boats along the waterfront.

While everyday life in the town is still based around fishing, tourism is becoming more and more important. Many residents now work in gift shops and restaurants. There are Internet cafés and a video-game company. Despite these modern changes, Lunenburg has maintained its history and charm. Its historic buildings, pretty scenery, museums, and festivals attract visitors every year.

Fishing Around the World

There are many rural fishing towns like Lunenburg all over the world. Their fishermen provide seafood for people every day. Fish and shellfish are sources of **nutrients** needed for health. In Japan, raw fish is served as sushi. In Spain, shellfish is a main part of a rice dish called paella. In Russia, people eat fish eggs as a spread called caviar.

▼ On the coast of India, local fishermen push their boat out to sea to catch fish to feed their village.

▲ Fishermen in the Pacific Ocean sometimes accidently catch sea turtles in their nets. Sea turtles are **endangered** animals. They must be put back into the water.

In parts of some seas and oceans, no fishing is allowed. This allows young fish and shellfish to grow and multiply and renew supplies of seafood. People who live in rural areas that once relied on fishing will now have to find new ways of getting everything they need.

Facts and Figures

How many?
Scientists have identified more than 100,000 different types of fish, crabs, lobsters, scallops, mussels, and clams living in the seas and oceans around the world.

The largest fish
The largest fish in the world is the whale shark. It can grow to more than 50 feet (14 meters) in length. That is longer than a school bus. It lives in warm seas and oceans.

The fishing industry
The United States is one of the largest fishing countries in the world. In Canada, there are more than 120,000 working fishermen and around 1,500 rural fishing communities.

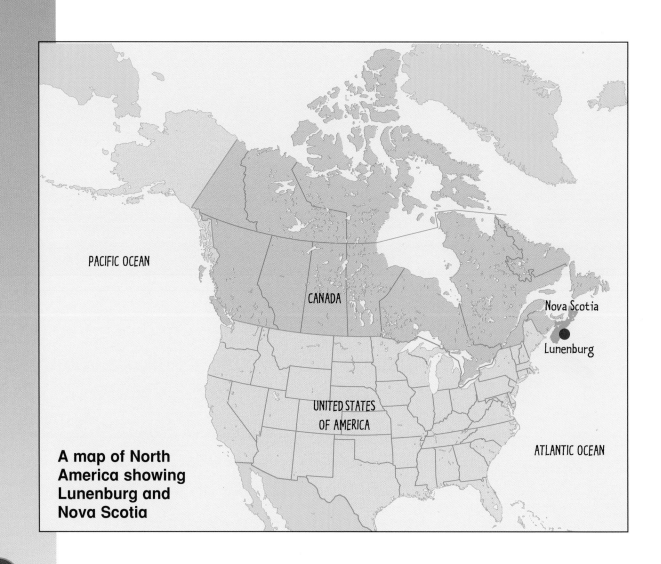

A map of North America showing Lunenburg and Nova Scotia

Glossary

angling Catching fish with a rod, line, and bait

aquaculture Raising mostly shellfish for food in artificial farms

bait Food to attract fish

city Large urban area, with thousands of people and many houses, offices, roads, and factories

commercial To do with buying and selling of goods and services

community A group of people who live, work, and play close together

crustacean Shellfish

dockers People who work along the waterfront at ports and harbors

endangered A living thing whose survival is threatened, often by human activity

energy The power to do work. It can come from burning fuels such as coal and oil, or from wind, water, and the Sun

factory A building where a lot of people work and make things

fish farm An artificial area set up along the coast where fish are grown to provide food

founded Started or set up something new

harbor A sheltered place where boats can load and unload. A large port can have many harbors

local People or place that is nearby

mollusk Type of sea creature with a soft body

molt To shed a shell or skin in order to grow a new one

navigate To find one's way, often with the help of maps or charts

nutrients Things in food that are needed for health, such as vitamins

processing Preparing, making ready, or changing into something useful

quota An agreed amount or number that sets a maximum limit on how many fish are caught each year or season

rakes Toothed brooms or shovels used to collect things by scraping

residents People who live in a place such as a village or apartment block

resources Things one needs or must have

rural A small, quiet living area in the countryside

town A place where people live that has many houses, roads, and stores, and maybe some offices and factories. Small towns can be rural, large towns are urban

tradition Something handed down through history

urban A built-up, busy area such as a city or big town

village A small rural area with a few houses

Further Information

Further Reading

Ridley, Frances. *Lost at Sea.* Crabtree Publishing Company, 2008
Hubbell, Patricia. *Boats: Speeding! Sailing! Cruising.* Marshall Cavendish, 2009
Bennet, Amy. *One Christmas in Lunenburg.* Lorimer, James & Company, 2004
Kurlansky, Mark. *The Cod's Tale.* Penguin, 2001

Web Sites

About Lunenburg
www.lunenburgns.com
www.explorelunenburg.ca/

Coloring Book
http://museum.gov.ns.ca/fma/new-frames-master.html
Download a free coloring book from the Fisheries Museum of the Atlantic

Cooking
www.highliner.com/site/eng/rec_kid.asp

Fishing
http://en.wikipedia.org/wiki/Fishing

Index

Printed in the U.S.A.—CG